Da Vinci Designs

by Kara Race-Moore

Editorial Offices: Glenview, Illinois • Parsippany, New Jersey • New York, New York
Sales Offices: Needham, Massachusetts • Duluth, Georgia • Glenview, Illinois
Coppell, Texas • Ontario, California • Mesa, Arizona

A Time of Rebirth

Renaissance means "rebirth." Historians use the term to describe the changes that happened in Europe from the 1300s through the 1500s. During the Renaissance, people in countries such as England, France, and Italy took on a new interest in the arts and sciences. They began exploring subjects people had not studied since the time of the ancient Greeks.

Leonardo da Vinci (1452–1519) lived during the Italian Renaissance. Keep reading to find out more about Leonardo da Vinci, the star of the Renaissance!

Self-portrait of Leonardo da Vinci

"Portrait of a bearded man, possibly a self-portrait" ca. 1513 by Leonardo da Vinci. Red chalk on paper. Biblioteca Reale, Turin, Italy.

A True Renaissance Man

Leonardo da Vinci was just one of many people whose works and ideas contributed to the Renaissance. Michelangelo, William Shakespeare, Galileo, Copernicus, and Johan Gutenberg all lived during the Renaissance! Shakespeare's plays, Gutenberg's printing press, and Galileo's and Copernicus's scientific discoveries changed the world.

These people **achieved** much. But none of them were Renaissance men in the way that da Vinci was. The term *Renaissance man* means someone who is talented in everything he does. Many consider da Vinci to be the most complete Renaissance man of all time.

This pendulum clock, originally designed by Galileo, was built in 1883.

Leonardo da Vinci had many different interests, but people mostly think of him as a painter. Da Vinci's *Mona Lisa* is one of the world's most famous paintings.

Da Vinci made his paintings as realistic as possible. Da Vinci also enjoyed studying nature. He often did realistic paintings of things from nature.

Artists like da Vinci made the Renaissance a golden age for painting. Michelangelo, a brilliant painter and sculptor, was da Vinci's biggest **rival.** They often competed for the same painting jobs. Many people argued over who was the better artist.

Mona Lisa by Leonardo da Vinci

"Mona Lisa," c. 1503–1506 by Leonardo da Vinci.
Oil on panel, 77 × 53 cm. Louvre, Paris, France.

How da Vinci Worked

More than anything, da Vinci wanted to understand how things worked. He believed that the only way to truly know something was by firsthand experience.

Da Vinci would start by observing events in the natural world. Then he would design experiments to find out what caused those events. Da Vinci would perform the experiments over and over. While experimenting he would take notes and draw sketches. Finally, da Vinci would take what he learned from his observations to form a conclusion. The result was a series of notebooks filled with sketches and details covering many fields of study. Da Vinci's notebooks spanned dozens of subjects, from archaeology to zoology.

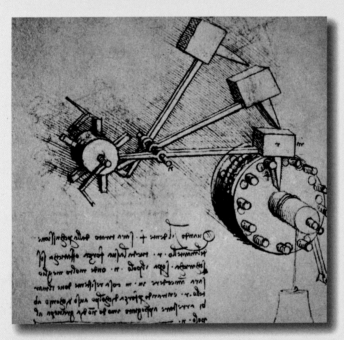

Da Vinci's sketch of parts of a clock

Da Vinci's Study of Anatomy

Da Vinci is also famous for his work in anatomy and physiology. Anatomy is the study of how the body is made. Physiology is the study of how the body works.

Da Vinci's love for mechanical designs carried over to his study of the human body. He drew detailed pictures of the human body and its parts. His notebooks included sketches of bones, muscles, organs, and blood vessels. Da Vinci drew the human body very carefully.

Da Vinci also studied mammals, birds, and amphibians. He compared each animal's features to those of other animals. Da Vinci made detailed notes and drawings of what he saw.

Da Vinci's drawing of the human torso showed some organs.

Da Vinci as Architect

Da Vinci was also a skilled **architect.** He designed churches, forts, and bridges. He had ideas for moving water through canals and aqueducts. Aqueducts are structures that let water flow from one area to another. Da Vinci designed a bridge that could be moved around, taken apart, and put back together.

One of da Vinci's boldest designs was for a bridge that would cross the Gulf of Istanbul. Engineers of the time said the bridge's weight would make it collapse. Modern engineers think that the bridge would have worked. As was often the case, da Vinci was ahead of his time.

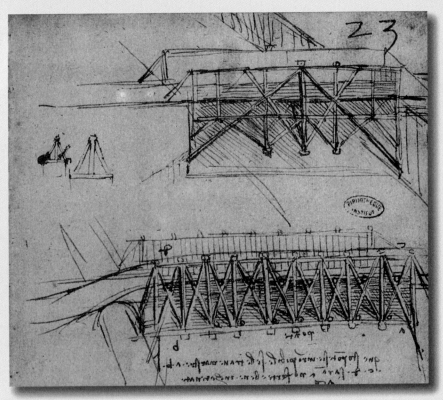

A sketch showing one of da Vinci's proposed bridges

Some of da Vinci's sketches of horses

At one point, da Vinci set out to create a **bronze** statue of a horse. It would be no ordinary statue. Da Vinci wanted to make it four times the size of an adult horse! Da Vinci prepared by studying horses. He made drawings of their bones and muscles. He also studied different metals and decided that bronze would work best.

Da Vinci made a clay model of the statue. He figured out the best way to melt the bronze that he would be using. But then war broke out between Italy and France. The clay statue was destroyed during a battle. The bronze intended for the statue was used to make ammunition for the **cannons.**

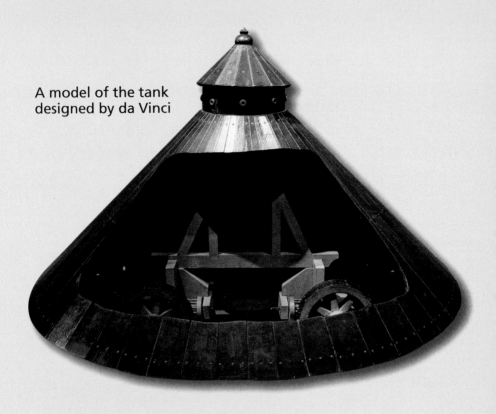

A model of the tank
designed by da Vinci

Da Vinci as Weapons Designer

When war broke out, the Italian government asked
da Vinci to design weapons. He designed new types of
cannons, catapaults, crossbows, and guns.

Da Vinci also invented completely new weapons. In his
notebooks, da Vinci had drawings of a multibarreled gun
and a mechanical bow.

One of the weapons that da Vinci designed was the
tank. With this idea, da Vinci was even more ahead of
his time than usual. It would take another four hundred
years before people figured out how to build tanks that ran
successfully!

Da Vinci was very good at making improvements on existing types of weapons. But da Vinci didn't like war. He would much rather study living things than design weapons. Da Vinci was a gentle person by nature. He would often buy caged birds at the market and set them free.

Da Vinci's dislike of war increased when he was designing tanks. He became afraid of trying to build a working tank. Da Vinci thought that tanks would make war even worse than it already was. Sadly, his fears were correct. Tanks have caused terrible destruction during modern wars.

Da Vinci's sketches of tank designs

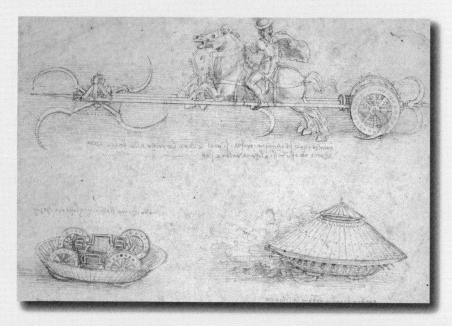

Putting Water to Work

Da Vinci observed water in all its forms. He noted how water changed as it got hotter or colder. To make it easier to study water, da Vinci made new equipment for doing water experiments.

Before people learned to use electricity, water was the main source of power. Waterwheels were used to power machines and do many different kinds of work. Ships traveled the rivers and seas, moving goods and ideas from place to place.

Da Vinci's study
of a waterwheel

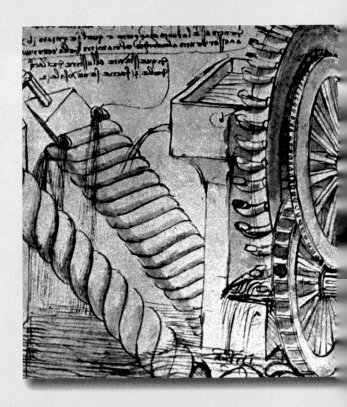

Da Vinci worked to invent things that would make it easier for people to use water. He came up with an early design for a life preserver. He also sketched devices that would let people breath underwater. And da Vinci came up with the idea of having people use webbed gloves to help them swim better.

Da Vinci designed an early type of submarine. He thought of new ways to attack ships underwater. Da Vinci also thought of ways to make ships' hulls stronger.

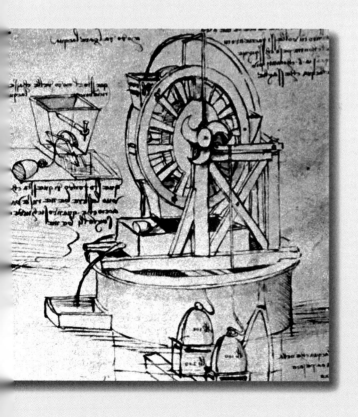

Da Vinci's Mind Takes to the Sky

Da Vinci was fascinated by the idea of flying. He thought he would become even more famous if he could find a way for humans to fly. To unlock the secret of flight, da Vinci studied wind currents and the flight patterns of flying creatures. He studied the wings of bats and birds, making many drawings of their shape and bone structure.

Da Vinci learned many things while studying bats and birds. He realized that their hollow bones made it easier for them to fly. Da Vinci figured out that there were many muscles in bats' and birds' bodies that helped them as they flew.

Da Vinci's drawing of a parachute

Da Vinci took what he learned from bats' and birds' wings to design wings that people could use. Nobody knows whether or not da Vinci ever **fashioned** any actual wings. But there is evidence that he made attempts to fly.

Da Vinci wrote that the best place to attempt to fly would be over a lake. That way the person trying to fly would land in the water instead of crashing into the ground. Da Vinci also wrote that the person trying to fly should wear a life preserver to avoid drowning.

Da Vinci also drew designs for parachutes and helicopters. It would take many years for those ideas to come to life. With his designs for flying machines, da Vinci again showed that he was centuries before his time.

Modern-day paratrooper

Da Vinci's Notebooks

Da Vinci never published his notes. After he died his amazing notebooks were scattered. Some of them disappeared. Then, in 1965, two of da Vinci's notebooks were found in the basement of the National Library in Madrid, Spain.

Da Vinci's notebooks are filled with many wonderful drawings, but his handwriting is hard to read. Da Vinci wrote backwards from right to left. He was left-handed, and he found it easier to write that way. This type of writing, called mirror script, can be read only when held up to a mirror.

Da Vinci's handwriting

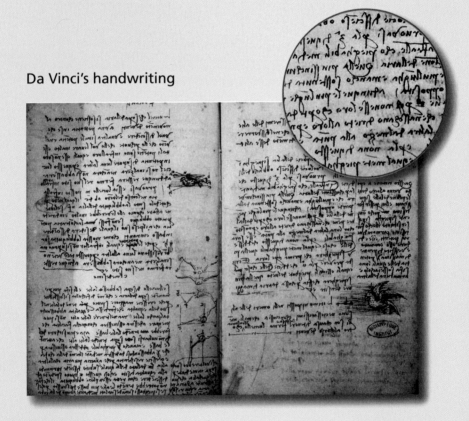

"Portrait of Francis I, King of France" by Jean Clouet, ca. 1530.

Da Vinci's Move to France

Da Vinci became **depressed** toward the end of his life. He was tired of living in Italy. The people there were only interested in his paintings. They did not care about his designs, inventions, and theories.

The French king, Francis I, helped da Vinci leave Italy. Why would a French person want to help da Vinci? After all, France and Italy were enemies. It had been French soldiers who had destroyed da Vinci's clay statue of a horse. But Francis liked da Vinci's paintings and admired his ideas. He wanted to bring the Renaissance to France. So he invited da Vinci to live in France.

Da Vinci accepted the king's offer. In France, da Vinci continued to paint, draw, and write down his ideas. He also had many discussions with King Francis, who liked hearing da Vinci's thoughts.

By the time he died in 1519, da Vinci was recognized throughout Europe as a genius. Da Vinci achieved incredible things. He was a brilliant **philosopher,** scientist, architect, engineer, and artist.

Da Vinci's drawings

As amazing as da Vinci was, he did have his flaws. His curiosity often got the better of him. For example, he would often drop one project he was in the **midst** of in order to work on another. People who paid da Vinci money to do paintings would get angry with him because he spent so much time on other things. Still, da Vinci was a Renaissance man. Whether it was painting the *Mona Lisa*, inventing the tank, or researching ways to fly, da Vinci could do it all!

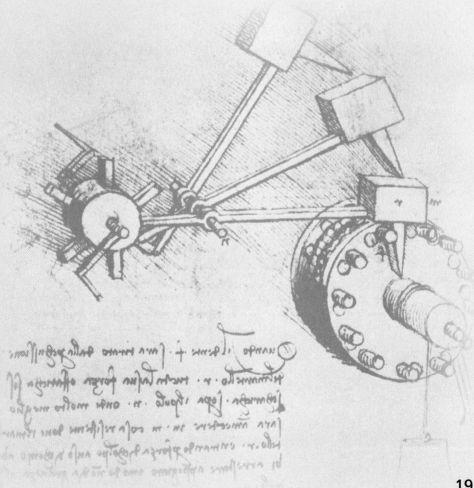

Glossary

achieved *v.* carried out to a successful end; accomplished; did

architect *n.* person who designs and makes plans for buildings

bronze *adj.* made of or similar in color to a dark yellow-brown alloy of copper and tin

cannons *n.* big guns, especially ones that are mounted on a base or wheels

depressed *adj.* gloomy; low-spirited; sad

fashioned *v.* made, shaped, or formed

midst *n.* the middle of

philosopher *n.* a person who attempts to discover and understand the basic nature of knowledge and reality

rival *n.* a person who wants and tries to get the same thing as another or who tries to equal or do better than another; competitor